I Am Just a Vessel

Toxic People!

Do *NOT* Play With Toxic People

Suzi Yelvington

TRILOGY CHRISTIAN PUBLISHERS

Tustin, CA

Trilogy Christian Publishers
A Wholly Owned Subsidiary of Trinity Broadcasting Network
2442 Michelle Drive
Tustin, CA 92780

I Am Just a Vessel: Toxic People!

Scripture quotations marked (KJV) are taken from the King James Version of the Bible. Public domain.

For information, address Trilogy Christian Publishing Rights Department, 2442 Michelle Drive, Tustin, CA 92780.

Trilogy Christian Publishing/ TBN and colophon are trademarks of Trinity Broadcasting Network.

For information about special discounts for bulk purchases, please contact Trilogy Christian Publishing.

Trilogy Disclaimer: The views and content expressed in this book are those of the author and may not necessarily reflect the views and doctrine of Trilogy Christian Publishing or the Trinity Broadcasting Network.

10 9 8 7 6 5 4 3 2 1

Library of Congress Cataloging-in-Publication Data is available.

ISBN: 979-8-89333-055-7

ISBN: 979-8-89333-056-4 (ebook)

Acknowledgments

I would like to acknowledge and thank Jenny Van Auken (Creative Director) and Trish Herndon (Graphic Designer) for their assistance and insight while working on this book.

Arguing with a fool only proves that there are two. Do not play with toxic people! Do not let the ugly in others kill the beautiful or handsome in you. Your diet is not only what you are eating. It also is what you watch, listen to, what you read, who you hang with. It is all about your mind, body, and soul man. You will be absolutely amazed at what you attract after you start believing in what you deserve. But you must do your part. You do not have to tolerate people who treat you poorly. This is all preparing you for your future. Also, learn to be okay with people not knowing your side of the story. It truly does not matter. God is in control anyway; keep moving. Trusting the Lord and doing good is the key. Just get out there and help others without telling the world what was wrong. "Taste and see that the Lord is good; blessed is the one who takes refuge in Him" (Psalm 34:8, NIV). Your greatest freedom ever is that you get to choose your own attitude. Write yourself a thank you note. What do you love about your life? Write out your three goals, and put on the attitude of excellence. Self-love is extremely powerful and contagious. Give it away!

Your secret to a happy life is giving God first part of your day. There is no secret to this. What you do in secret with God, He will bless you for in public. This is your priority for every decision in your life for true success. Do not disturb. I love the morning most of all. It is time to get focused. The opinions of others will never cut you a check. Only grow apart from people who are not growing. You cannot force anyone to see you are a blessing; you just must let them miss out. Some people come into your life to teach you how to let go. Let the Lord fight your battles; He has not lost one yet. Get your Holy Spirit fire back. Do not let anyone disrespect you. I am okay with being misunderstood. Declare: I will respond and not react. I enjoy time alone. I set boundaries. I am in the healing mode over my body, mind, and soul, through mighty prayer. Try this again, this time with God. I am loved. I am gifted. I am unique. I am confident. My secret is simple: I PRAY. This is tough, but so am I. "But as for you, be strong and do not give up, for your work will be rewarded" (2 Chronicles 15:7, NIV). Let all that you do be done in love.

You are bigger than what is making you anxious. The same boiling water that softens the potato hardens the egg. It is all about what you are made of, not the circumstances. Haters, like parrots, talk much, but they cannot fly. Eagles say nothing but conquer the skies. Haters also broadcast your failures and will whisper your success. Pressure creates diamonds. I used to care what others thought about me, until I realized they do not pay my bills. Know what you bring to the table in a humble way. You cannot fix others by breaking them down. Know yourself. Have you ever met a hater doing better than you? God promises to make something good out of the storks that bring devastation to your life. "And we know that in all things God works for the good of those who love him, who have been called according to his purpose" (Romans 8:28, NIV).

Declare: I thoroughly enjoy minding my own business. A private life is a happy life. If it does not involve you, it should not concern or control you. It is no secret. Truth sounds like hate to those who hate truth. Sometimes others try to expose your wrong. That is okay. Make sure you do not start seeing yourself through the eyes of those who do not value you or are jealous of you! Money cannot buy you. Manners, morals, integrity, class, character, respect, common sense, trust, patience, your faith, or having the power of the Holy Spirit living inside of you—all these take managing yourself. Give God your weakness, and he will give you His strength in all the areas you are weak. Manage your emotions. They will trick you and mess you up. Let every situation be what it is! Not what you think it should be. If you do not like something, take away its only power: YOUR ATTENTION! Whenever you feel unloved, unimportant, or insecure, remember to whom YOU belong. "Consequently, you are no longer foreigners and strangers but fellow citizens with God's people and members of his household, built on the foundation of the apostles and prophets, with Christ Jesus himself as the chief cornerstone. In him the whole building is joined together and rises to become a holy temple in the Lord. And in him you too are being built together to become a dwelling in which God lives by his Spirit" (Ephesians 2:19-22, NIV).

If you want to know how rich you are, look at how much you have of things money just cannot buy. Learn to worship God in all that you do have. Someone somewhere is waiting on you to display what God has created you to do. The world has enough men and women who know how to dress and do their make-up and hair. This life needs men and women who know how to do hard and holy things. Never be the reason someone asks God for peace. God forgive me for the times I have been the toxic person in someone's life. There are times you must let people know it is not a grudge you are holding. They are boundaries you are keeping in a place of peace. The gospel is the only story where our Hero dies for the villain. Everything you need is already inside of you. Stop searching for someone to light your fire. Getting older may weaken your vision, but you can see through people more clearly. "Be completely humble and gentle; be patient, bearing with one another in love" (Ephesians 4:2, NIV).

Be humble enough to know you and I are both far from perfect. Stay confident enough to know you can do all things through Christ. "And we know that in all things God works for the good of those who love Him, who have been called according to his purpose" (Romans 8:28, NIV). Recognize what is important and create boundaries. Trust God. Stay around people who talk about visions and ideas, not those who talk about others. Women and men with ambition run their business, not their mouths. Invest in ideas and businesses, not in emotions and other people's drama. If you find your passion, Monday will be your favorite day of the week. Be humble. If you look at the people in your circle and don't get inspired, you don't have a circle of influence. A glowing person can help other people glow. Pay attention. One person's success can only help another person's success. Stay strong in the Lord. Your daily habits, good or bad, will define your future.

Note this: There's nothing as blinding to one's soul as bitter jealousy. Winners focus on winning. Losers focus on the winners. Envy eats up your own beauty. Pay attention; you will see it. Envy is a form of hatred built on insecurity. I pray we all make it to success in life. Your spiritual maturity is when you have the power to destroy someone with the truth, but you breathe instead and walk away and let God handle your battles. Live healthy. Stay positive and do not give up. The Bible says, "For where you have envy and selfish ambition, there you will find disorder and every evil practice" (James 3:16, NIV). The envious are a torment to themselves. Anger, fear, and insecurities fuel jealousy. Guard your heart. A peaceful heart leads to a healthy body. "Therefore encourage one another and build each other up, just as in fact you are doing" (1 Thessalonians 5:11, NIV). There are thirty Bible verses on envy.

THINGS to REMEMBER to protect your PEACE. Love with strength. Sometimes we just need a quick prayer to help us through the day! Life will always offer you a second chance. It is called TOMORROW. Bloom like you have your own season. Do not take things personally; miserable people do miserable things. Let success be your noise, not your mouth. Stop letting the behavior of others ruin your peace. Never underestimate God's hand over all your plans. If it is God's will, it will be. God knows best. God is going to show out, not only for your destiny but to prove to others around that the Lord is for you and not against you. God is greater than the giants you face. Take that rest in knowing you are fearfully and wonderfully made. "Before a word is on my tongue you, Lord, know it completely" (Psalm 139:4, NIV). You deserve words that make you smile every day. WORDS that remind you how valuable you are. Breathe.

It is just not elegant at all to gossip about other bodies or appearances. Manners still matter. Hold your posture up. Spend time with successful people. Be responsible for your own life. Engage in eye contact when talking. Self-discipline is knowing everything in life is about taking balance. Be present. How you dress is how you are addressed. Don't respond to rude nonsense comments. Don't make a promise you can't keep. Be polite to everyone. Don't speak curse words. Don't be jealous. *Stop* comparing yourself to other people! Doing that invites condemnation, not from the Lord. You are very unique, like no other. We cannot even compare our struggles. You may not even be aware of what others are truly going through. God will not help you live someone else's life. He created you on purpose for His purpose. God will always lead you into triumph. Less is more. Be stronger than your excuses. Know what you bring to the table. Keep your lives free from the love of money, and be content with what you have, because God has said, "Never will I leave you; never will I forsake you" (Hebrews 13:5, NIV). Lord, teach me what I can't see. But first, PRAY.

Your manners are your strength and beauty. Being a good person will not guarantee that others will be good to you. You will always and only have complete control over yourself and how you choose to be as a person. The most important relationship is with the Lord and yourself. Disconnecting from certain people will bless your life more than you know. SOMETIMES, you must remain silent because no words can explain what you see. PRAYER WORKS. "And I will do whatever you ask in my name so that the Father may be glorified in the Son. You may ask me for anything in my name, and I will do it" (John 14:13-14, NIV). The grass is greener where you water it. God can. But first, thank God for what he has already done. Those who kneel before God can stand before anyone. It is time to get focused. DOUBT BUSTER: Read God's Word. "Consequently, faith comes from hearing the message, and the message is heard through the word about Christ" (Romans 10:17, NIV). Make this day count. Each day you must choose either the pain of discipline or the pain of regret. You will never have this day again—make it count.

NOTHING will bring you greater peace than minding your own business. People spend time in others business when they should spend time correcting their own. Don't study others; you won't graduate. If you do not understand the whole situation, we do not have the right to have a finger-pointing opinion. Negative people need drama like oxygen. Stay positive; it always will take their breath away. Do not listen to unfair criticism—just blood, sweat, and tears. Do not be mad at someone because someone else is. Earned, not given. Real people mind their own business. Respect people's privacy. It's just none of your business. Caring about what people think is useless. Most people do not really know what they think of themselves. And you are seriously going to be hurt over the opinions of others? Do your best, and God will do the rest. "No one will be able to stand against you all the days of your life. As I was with Moses, so I will be with you; I will never leave you nor forsake you" (Joshua 1:5, NIV). Sometimes you just must look at all the moving parts. Pray for wisdom.

Avoiding certain people to protect your mental health is not a weakness. IT IS WISDOM. Transition. Life is so beautiful when you spend it with people who make your heart happy. Your purpose anyways is not to gain approval but to be SALT and LIGHT in others' lives. Train yourself right now to take nothing personally. Socially distance yourself from people who harm your mental health, people who act like a victim in problems they created. Your degree is a piece of paper; your education is seen in your behavior. When the Enemy starts knocking on a door you closed long ago, just say: "Jesus, it's for you."

"Praise be to the Lord, to God our Savior, who daily bears our burdens" (Psalm 68:19, NIV). The damage no longer controls your life. Hallelujah!

This is just for YOU! WORRY-FREE. You are special. Every day is a second chance. You need to accept yourself. You do not need to be accepted by others. This is a reminder to just believe. Wasted time is worse than wasted money. Turn your pain into power. Happiness is a way of life. Confidence is silent. Do not make things more difficult than they need to be. "And we know that all things work together for good to them that love God, to them who are called according to His purpose. Study the Word because the enemy is studying you. Go back and tell Hezekiah, the ruler of my people, 'This is what the LORD, the God of your father David, says: I have heard your prayer and seen your tears; I will heal you. On the third day from now you will go up to the temple of the LORD" (2 Kings 20:5, NIV). Be the person you would love to look up to. Be grateful for your life. Do not worry. He is in control.

You are supposed to fail sometimes. It's a required part of life. Sometimes you must make a decision that may hurt your heart, but it will heal your soul. Manners are beautiful and handsome. Silence is luxurious. Feelings don't work on a timetable. Prayer works. "And I will do whatever you ask in my name, so that the Father may be glorified in the Son. You may ask me for anything in my name, and I will do it" (John 14:13-14, NIV). Believe that God will do the impossible in your life. While others are hoping you will fall, stay praying they will get up on their feet. "Blessed are the pure in heart, for they will see God at work. A person with class is always timeless. Do NOT be overcome by evil but overcome evil with good" (Romans 12:21, NIV). Confident people are not desperate for attention. We are all going through life for the first time. Those things others say about you, say more about them. Declare: "For he will command his angels concerning you to guard you in all your ways" (Psalm 91:11, NIV). Become your own best friend. Know your worth.

It's a must. STOP telling people your business. Some talk to you so they can talk about you. Complaining and belly aching and fearing all open the door to demonic activity! Fluttering around acting like you're in control is a trick of Satan!

Humbleness, worshipping when it makes no sense unlocks the favor of God over everything you set out to do! The ones who are jealous? They don't want what you have; they just don't want you to have it. Read that again. Let's stop a moment and pray for the world. Pray for our nation. "But when you pray, go into your room, close the door and pray to your Father, who is unseen. Then your father, who sees what is done in secret, will reward you" (Matthew 6:6, NIV). Today let your faith be bigger than your fears. Let the power of His presence quiet all your fears today. "Humble yourselves, therefore, under God's mighty hand, that he may lift you up in due time" (1 Peter 5:6, NIV). Teach us to do your will, Lord. Our world is in desperate need. We are powerless; our confidence is in God who is thoroughly able. Prayer is the best thing we can do together. Pray that souls will be saved. Pray for laborers. Prayer is powerful!

One beautiful day, you will reach a point where you are no longer available trying to convince others how you feel about situations. If you know your truth and what you have done, that is all that matters. Be set free. Remember this: No one changes unless they want to. Only one thing makes anyone change: their own realization that they need to. When you allow the wrong people in your life, stuff comes up missing quickly. Like peace, hope, joy, love, faith, future, time. Yes, the wrong people steal these things from your good heart. Peace and blessings over your home now. God removes people from your life; let them go and keep on moving, for greater is coming. When the world beats you down, open your Bible. Stop emotional vampires in your life. Happiness is an inside job and your responsibility. Read Philippians 4:8, Galatians 5:22, Psalm 1:1-3, and Ephesians 6:10-20. This is how we fight our battles. Those who say it costs nothing to be kind haven't met a narcissistic. Be aware.

Your healing process is your responsibility. It will not be a bubble bath. It is getting to the root of your deadly emotions. I pray you do not spend your life feeling sorry for yourself all the time. Live with God's purpose and set boundaries. Look back at where you came from; feel good so far about that process. Declare: The damage no longer controls me. You are not weak just because your heart feels so heavy. Do not go back to what tried to damage you. Forgiving yourself is just as important as forgiving others. Each scar is a beautiful reminder of what you have overcome. These lessons in life—you cannot afford to learn them again. When love is real… "Love is patient, love is kind. It does not envy, it does not boast, it is not proud. It does not dishonor others, it is not self-seeking, it is not easily angered, it keeps no record of wrongs. Love does not delight in evil but rejoices with the truth. It always protects, always trusts, always hopes, always perseveres" (1 Corinthians 13:4-7, NIV). Your wound may not be your fault, but your healing is your responsibility. Don't look for perfect, look for honest.

If someone around you leaves you with confused feelings of uncomfortableness and uncertainty and a battle in your mind, you need the Holy Spirit to guide you through prayer. Healthy relationships are difficult for wounded people. Some people think if they do not support you, you will fail. Declare: I will remain focused on my goals. Even with difficulty I will not give up. I know I will make it with the Lord by my side. Things are getting better. No problem will stop me. Repeat daily. Journal three things you are grateful for. "All things are possible with God. I have given you authority to trample on snakes and scorpions and to overcome all the power of the enemy; nothing will harm you" (Luke 10:19, NIV). Crave peace. Stop allowing negativity in your life. Labor of love.

I am a champion. Think about this. It is what you do in your free time that will set you free or enslave you. And the choice is yours. You can have results or excuses—not both. Keep your mind right with the Word of God, your soul filled with the Holy Spirit, and your heart strong with agape love. Repeat to yourself. Stay away from victim blaming. Recovery Tip: Let go of the urge to make a narcissistic accountable for their behavior; they think they have never done anything wrong. Be set free today in the Lord. "For the battle is not yours but God's" (2 Chronicles 20:15, NIV). Be thankful for the struggle because, without it, you would not have stumbled across your strength. Design the life you love.

This is a TEST. This is one thing the Lord is requesting and requires of us: to walk with God in humility. "He has shown you, O mortal, what is good. And what does the Lord require of you? To act justly and to love mercy and to walk humbly you're your God" (Micah 6:8, NIV). This will be the most difficult virtue to grow in. You must not consider yourself more highly than others, not superior to anyone else either. We must have and desire a humble heart. It is not an attitude of entitlement and believes everything is an undeserved gift from God. Everything is a beautiful blessing. You won't complain, criticize, or murmur about your life or anyone else's either. No envy or jealousy—that's wickedness. We need to endure what we are going through with a happy attitude and heart. A positive attitude is a must. We must think and treat others well and speak well about their lot in life. The Lord has shown me what is good. Practice kindness and compassion. If someone complains about you, gaslights you, finger points, you need new friends. One bad apple can spoil the whole bushel. Who are you listening to today?

I pray, my friends, that you get through battles you do not talk about, in Jesus' name. Pray more; worry less. Toxic people condition you to believe that the problem is not abuse but, instead, that your reactions to them are the real problem. This is why we need the supernatural wisdom from the Holy Spirit. Make no mistake: You won't think right without Him. Declare: "Do not conform to the pattern of this world but be transformed by the renewing of your mind. Then you will be able to test and approve what God's will is-his good, pleasing and perfect will" (Romans 12:2, NIV). For I am fearfully and wonderfully made by Him. Pray for people to keep your name out of their pity-party conversations. Declare: Lord, please help me to stand firm in my faith. Do not blame a clown for acting like a clown. Stop going to the circus. Walk away from disagreements that will never be resolved. God's got this. Go after your dreams, not people.

Secrets in life can and will make you sick. Get them into God's marvelous light. The truth of God's word will set you free. Get to the root of your secret! Get set free. You and I cannot go on this way, even if it is from your childhood. No shame—it must bow and flee. Do not internalize it one more day. Envy and bitterness are a root. It must be plucked out. Ask God to show you if you feel like there is something wrong. You may not have this, but someone close to you may be suffering. A hard heart and a miserable attitude are from not trusting God. God will come through for you. You must love yourself in order to love others. People find things wrong with others because they find so much stuff wrong with themselves. Change. Your success remains in working on yourself by trusting God. Fight like God fights with his love and his Word. Attitude is everything. Stop spraying perfume or Lysol where it stinks, and get busy cleaning up—including our hearts! It's time. It is A NEW SEASON to birth your dream by cleaning up with the Holy Ghost. Refuse to live in deception. Imagine if our world got together to pray against all the mess.

Stay prayed up. Every time you forgive, you disappoint the Enemy. Declare: Every demonic arrow released against my life, go back and destroy the camp of the Enemy in Jesus' name. A determined person does not find it hard to succeed. They find it hard to stop trying. Believe me: God can get YOU through anything. A negative mind will never give you a positive life. No longer a slave to fear, I am a child of God. We all know someone who speaks fluent nonsense. Declare: It's my winning season! Your declarations are your manifestations for your future. You can face your trials with God's confidence. How many wounds have you turned into wisdom? Never forget your own worth. To some you can do one thousand powerful things. But they focus on the one thing that doesn't fit into their needs. Those are NOT your responsibility or people. Give yourself permission to move on. I am thankful for all the difficult people in my life. They have SHOWN me exactly what I do not want to be. Praise Jesus. When your attentions are pure, you don't lose anyone—they lose you.

Sometimes you must disconnect and enjoy your own peace. Do not be a prisoner of past opinions, past choices. It is always a great lesson. It is not a life sentence. Stand outside of arguments. OUTSTANDING. Always share your spirit of excellence. Cancel all subscriptions to others' drama. Never stop learning. Only compete with yourself. Some should use a glue stick instead of Chapstick. "'For I know the plans I have for you,' declares the Lord, 'plans to prosper you and NOT to harm you plans to give you hope and a future'" (Jeremiah 29:11, NIV). Declare the Word. The Enemy is fighting you because you're strong. God is not finished with you yet. Trust the Holy Spirit. If you feel alone, remember God is with you. God is asking you to trust Him.

One of the most powerful and precious gifts that the Lord offers every one of us is the Word of God. Receive and recite God's Word, and you watch it change your whole entire life. "But mark this: There will be terrible times in the last days. People will be lovers of themselves, lovers of money, boastful, proud, abusive, disobedient to their parents, ungrateful, unholy, without love, unforgiving, slanderous, without self-control, brutal, not lovers of the good, treacherous, rash, conceited, lovers of pleasure rather than lovers of God – having a form of godliness but denying its power. Have nothing to do with such people" (2 Timothy 3:1-5, NIV). God's Word changes us. Be faithful and determined all the way through this journey of life to see victory and to enjoy every step of the way. Keep your faith strong and stand—keys for that victorious life. You must choose to have a positive healthy mindset daily. Choose!

It is not your job to figure out why others do not like you. You are not their therapist. All you need right now is know they do not care for you or like you, and you need to move forward. Do not spend endless years on trying to prove who you are. If they do not get it by now, they never will. God knows what he is doing. He has it all planned out, not to abandon you, plans for hope, joy, and future. Declare: I believe God's got it all worked out. It is just a matter of his time. He knows all your thoughts, all your intentions, and all the wonderful seeds you have planted helping others out at the workplace and hospitality. He holds the keys to new doors and your future. You cannot ever fool God. Others may have a story and fool others, but they just cannot fool God. The Bible does say: "You pick what you plant" (Galatians 6:7). "Be not deceived" (Proverbs 14:14-16). You harvest what you plant, whether good or bad. So be extra careful. Read Proverbs 14. POWERFUL. It is healthy to be content, but envy will eat you up.

Don't be the perfect one; be the right person. God can do amazing things with a willing heart. God is not mad at you (Psalm 145:8). Teach your mind to respect your body. Remember: Difficult does not mean impossible. Do not let people bring you down. Overcome problems together. Confidence is not, "They will not like me." Confidence is, "I'll be fine if they don't." God didn't give you this life to waste it. Others may laugh because they have no idea what you're capable of. God has anointed you with his favor. If they do not know you personally, do not take it personally. Don't chase. "But you are a chosen people, a royal priesthood, a holy nation, God's special possession, that you may declare the praises of him who called you out of darkness into his wonderful light" (1 Peter 2:9, NIV). God's Special Possession. Mercy & Grace.

Sometimes you must make that decision that will hurt your heart, but it will heal your soul. No one is strong enough to tear down what God is building. Declare that out loud. My greatest hobby is minding my own business, and I love it there. It is not the stab in the back that hurts! It is when you turn around and see who is holding the knife. That blessing you waited for is about to arrive. Stay patient your comeback is stronger than that setback. Forgive people, so you can move on. Do not waste your time on worry. Use your time to believe, create, trust, grow, and heal. God is always on time. Trust Him. That blessing you prayed for is on the way. Every season serves a purpose. Ecclesiastes 3 tells us to enjoy the present, no matter what!

Do not beg or convince others to choose you. Our God is too big and has a beautiful plan over your life. Get set free today. It is what it is! Do not get mad. Do not get even. Rise above it all. Become so engaged in your spiritual maturity growth that you forget all the bad things that have happened. Appreciate the things that are molding you into a better person. Even if it has hurt you and you do not understand it, you need it for whom God is making you become. It is so empowering to say, "This is not serving me or my goals" and just walk away happy. Focus on Bible knowledge. Focus on Holy Spiritual growth. Focus on growing as a person. Then the right people will find you. God has a plan. Declare: I am the designer of my future when I put God first in all I do. "Remain in me, as I also remain in you. No branch can bear fruit by itself; it must remain in the vine. Neither can you bear fruit unless you remain in me" (John 15:4, NIV). God's direction is more important than speed. Personal growth in God.

S tay focused on your God-given goals, and you will not get distracted. Imagine the person you want to become and be that. Funny when you do not let people disrespect you, they start calling you difficult. Be the ruthless editor of your own life and what you allow in your home. When God opens a door, no one can shut it. The only person you need to impress is yourself. Work on you. Learn to be satisfied with others not knowing the other side of the situation. You have nothing to prove to others; please be set free. That one day I finally discovered my strength in God and the whole game changed. Hallelujah. "Love is kind. It is not rude. Love does not delight in evil but rejoices with the truth" (1Corinthians 13:6, NIV). Jesus, he is as close as the mention of his name. Do not underestimate the POWER of consistency and desire.

Bless them well and move on. Publicly thank God for all the things He is doing privately. Praise you, Lord. Avoiding certain people to protect your mental health is not a weakness. It is WISDOM. Examine what you have tolerated. Whatever you are not changing, you are choosing. Those who kneel before God will stand before anyone. "What, then, shall we say in response to these things? If God is for us, who can be against us?" (Romans 8:31, NIV). We will repeat what we won't repair. Toxic people will make you feel like you're holding a grudge. No, it is called boundaries. Clutter is nothing more than postponing decision making. Best advice: Mind your own business. If you won't ask for their advice, stop excepting their opinions. Our world can be changed by our faith example. Never wrestle with others. You both get dirty, and they will love it. Mind your own business. A lack of boundaries invites the lack of respect. Read that again. It takes God's grace to remain kind in those cruel situations.

He whom the Son sets free is free indeed (John 8:36). "Stay joy-filled. Finally, brothers and sisters, whatever is true, whatever is noble, whatever is right, whatever is pure, whatever is lovely, whatever is admirable-if anything is excellent or praiseworthy-think about such things" (Philippians 4:8, NIV). Whatever you are not changing, you are choosing. Boundaries are the key! Without talking or badmouthing. Just do it and become a person of excellence! I am set free! Declare it! It's called operating out of your higher nature, which is spiritual maturity you get by seeking the supernatural power of the Holy Spirit DAILY to renew your mind. (Romans 12:2). We are all being distracted by other issues and situations we all get dragged in. It is done on purpose by the devil. We need to rise above the noise and get set free from things that do not concern us; we need to guard our gates. Eyes, ears, and mouth! Especially working with so many others! It is a must for spiritual maturity!

The Lord showed me last week to be a ruthless editor of my life. The reason why we don't get answers or breakthrough is because we are infiltrated with others' stuff. We need to insulate our minds, hearts, and tongues with the powerful Word of God—not others' weak words. That is poisonous to our prayers!

You are the designer of your future; why are you explaining your absence to someone who has failed to appreciate your presence? Toxic people create chaos, point fingers, shift blame, never take responsibility for their rude behavior. This is your life, and that is the only explanation you will ever need. If it is not nourishing your soul, let it go so you can glow. If you keep looking for that one person that will change your life, look in the mirror. Being raised right is how you treat people, your manners, your respect. People who invest in themselves go further in life and with others too. If you know you can do better, then do better. If you are living Galatians 5:22 in the way of the Holy Spirit, expect good things, because you have planted good seeds. You deserve the affection that you keep pouring into others.

P.S. Always make room for more beauty in your God-given life. The day I met the Lord, my whole life changed. My first thought in the morning is always God.

G rowing up in spiritual maturity, I have realized I pray not to be around drama, conflict, or negativity. Quickly remove yourself from people who treat you like your time does not matter, like your feelings are worthless, or like your soul is replaceable. Declare: Holy Spirit, cleanse me from anything that breaks your heart. Be so rooted in the Word of God that nobody's absence or presence can disturb your inner peace. Practice makes perfect peace. Trusting the Holy Spirit is looking to the future with great excitement. I believe He is going to work out everything for His good, just for you (Romans 8:28). Stand on this promise over you and your house. What you give power to has power over you. Dove or the raven? The Dove is the supernatural Holy Spirit. The raven is the flesh. Which one will you listen to? Protector, our light in the darkness, our keys to the future are all held by the Holy Spirit. The raven is believing in the flesh to provide protection, be the light, hold the key for them. I will put all my trust in the SUPERNATURAL, not the flesh, for my future. My peace is more important than reacting to something that doesn't deserve my emotions.

B eing a nice person also means being nice to yourself as well. That's why healthy boundaries are so important to your well-being. Sometimes you must give up on people, not because you do not care but because you see they don't. The words you SPEAK become the house you live in. "The tongue has the power of life and death, and those who love it will eat its fruit" (Proverbs 18:21, NIV). That is how you grow in the supernatural Holy Spirit. Once a week even ask yourself: What am I taking for granted? Gratitude is a key. Make peace with your broken pieces. Adjust your life to the absence of others instead of adjusting your boundaries for your health. Do not accommodate disrespect. Leave that right there. No need to belly ache about negativity. Adjust and do more Bible study; see what the Holy Spirit has in store to protect your heart and grow in the Holy Spirit. No doubt, no fear. There is only one foundation; we believe in the Holy Spirit, and he will give us new life. I learned a long time ago the wisest thing I can do is be on my own side of growing in Him, because some will hold grudges against you for things they did. Pray for spiritual discernment and keep it to yourself. May the flowers remind us why the rain is so necessary.

D o not let any human weakness have power over you, causing you to be separated from God. "Direct my footsteps according to your word; let no sin rule over me" (Psalm 119:133, NIV). Declare: Establish my footsteps, Lord. Reading the Word is wise, but meditating and devoting our thoughts to it is a superpower and supernatural from God. Choose a scripture that speaks to you; get into a habit of speaking it out loud throughout your day. This is how it will get rooted into your thinking and speaking. Soon and very soon, it changes you from the inside out. Devote your time to the Word, and the world cannot devour your mind, body, or soul. If anyone has come against you with a lie or an exaggeration, just remember that battle belongs to the Lord. No need to defend yourself; the Lord knows everything and sees everything. No worries. Trust the outcome. It is more trying to stay humble during success in life than it is in failure. Allow the Holy Spirit to bless your life with truth. Read the Word. It will unclutter all the idle chatter. "I rise before dawn and cry for help; I have put my hope in your word. My eyes stay open through the watches of the night, that I may meditate on your promises" (Psalm 119:147-148, NIV). There is a hidden treasure in reading the Word. While seeking advice from wise people is not wrong, we should be mature enough in our faith that we don't run to others every time we need to know what to do in situations. Rev it up!

D on't let the ugly in others kill the BEAUTY in you. Let God deal with your enemies. "The Lord will fight for you; you need only to be still" (Exodus 14:14, NIV). "But I will restore you to health and heal your wounds, declares the Lord, because you are called an outcast, Zion for whom no one cares" (Jeremiah 30:17, NIV). Haters will always discredit your hard work, when they have done nothing. Keep going. Real people won't pick apart your success. God is such a gentleman, he's always opening doors. "I consider that our present sufferings are not worth comparing with the glory that will be revealed in us" (Romans 8:18, NIV). There will be many chapters in your life. Do not get stuck in the one you are in now. A jealous spirit will cause you to mistreat people who could have been a blessing to you. Pray on it. Pray over it. Pray through it. You are about to thank God for the process. Examine what you tolerate. Holy Spirit, you are welcome here!

A break from someone will make you realize how much you truly miss them or how much peace you have without them. If it is not from God, I will gladly wait. Invest in ideas and business, not in emotions of people. I won't tear anyone down that badmouths; they are already down. Pray for them—that's better. Worship while you wait. God will make a way. DON'T QUIT. God is about to do something big. Radical breakthrough. Confusion to the camp of the Enemy. The drama-mobile runs on attention. Stop giving it fuel. But it is your behavior that will reveal your true character. Being determined is the golden ticket. Any fool can criticize, condemn, and love to complain, and most do. "Now to him who can do immeasurably more than all we ask or imagine, according to his power that is at work within us" (Ephesians 3:20, NIV). Believe it. Our thinking vs. God's promises.

Detoxing from unhealthy relationships is a process, and it will take time. Pray for supernatural wisdom from God's Word. We are all going through life for the first time. "He heals the brokenhearted and binds up their wounds" (Psalm 147:3, NIV)." For he will command his angels concerning you to guard you in all your ways" (Psalm 91:11, NIV). An ugly spirit cancels out a pretty face. If another's absence brings you peace, you didn't lose them; God shifted them. Every day, STAND GUARD at the door of your mind. That's the key for your life. Don't put your key to your life in anyone else's pocket. Pray. He listens. Choose people who are good for your mental health and don't finger point. Do not seek revenge on anyone; most of them are already miserable. Drama is done out of pure jealousy. Boundaries protect your heart and mind. "He gives strength to the weary and increases the power of the weak" (Isaiah 40:29, NIV). "But he was pierced for our transgressions, he was crushed for our iniquities; the punishment that brough us peace was on him, and by his wounds we are healed" (Isaiah 53:5, NIV). You are special—

yes, you. "Those who seek the Lord shall not lack any good thing" (Psalm 34:10) Mistreating people who love and adore God is a dangerous thing.

The ultimate enemy of the Lord is the spirit of pride. Pride is what kicked Satan out of heaven and one day into hell. What is pride? It says: "You're always right. You don't need anyone. You don't need help. You've got this on your own." That's not the sound of God's voice. Pride wants to be number one not number two, and it always wants more. Declare it out loud: "If my people, who are called by my name, will HUMBLE THEMSELVES and pray and seek my face and turn from their wicked ways, then I will hear from heaven, and I will forgive their sin and heal their land" (2 Chronicles 7:14, NIV). Choose humility over pride. Pride is the ultimate enemy towards God. We are forgiven and healed. Pride is a voice not from God. Holy Spirit, you are welcome here!

Grudges are for those who insist that they are owed something. Forgiving, however, is for those who are already blessed, and they know it to move on. People at war with themselves always cause damage in the lives of those around them. Extremely toxic people usually select a few close to them so their bad behavior won't be found out. I only grow apart from people who don't grow. Pay attention how people act when you are not on good terms. Having a boundary is not a grudge. "Above all else, guard your heart, for everything you do flows from it" (Proverbs 4:23, NIV). Don't get overwhelmed, the Lord supports you with his hand. "Though he may stumble, he will not fall, for the Lord upholds him with his hand" (Psalm 37:24, NIV). Never be a prisoner of your past. Don't compare your life to others. Judge no one. Just improve yourself. Your life right now is a result of your decisions. Daily faith reminders. You are never too young to start a purpose, never too old to chase a new dream.

If you really want closure at some point, you may have to shut that door. Your past is just part of your life story, and you need to know it has NO POWER over you. The past is where you learned the lesson. In your new future is where you nicely apply that lesson learned. Do not lose your present, a gift from God to your past. One of the most toxic things I have ever done was ignoring the bad in someone I thought I was in love with. You can only move on once you accept what is gone! God is your father; you are his child. Stay grateful for every day presents called life, for amazing benefits called blessings, and for your reward called ETERNAL Life. "Praise be to the Lord, to God our Savior, who daily bears our burdens" (Psalm 68:19, NIV). Blessed be the Lord, who daily loads us with his benefits, even the God of our salvation. SELAH. Successful people make decisions based on where they want to be in life!

Prayer for Salvation

If you need Jesus and want a personal relationship with Him, pray this very simple prayer out loud...

"Father God, I love you. I believe in you. I need you. I am sorry for my sins. I am sorry about the way I've lived. I am sorry for shutting you out. I want you in my life. I surrender. I yield. I receive Jesus as my Savior and my Lord. I believe He died for me. He rose from the dead. He's alive today. Come into me. Take me just the way I am. Now make me everything you want me to be. I believe I'm saved. I'm on my way to heaven, and I'm going to enjoy the trip.

In Jesus' Name, Amen."